HIGH SCORE

What is NPS and Why is it Important?

Net Promoter Score (NPS) serves as a powerful beacon to measure customer loyalty and satisfaction, focusing on the pivotal question: how likely are you to recommend a product or service to others? This insightful metric categorizes responses on a scale of 0 to 10 into three groups: promoters (scores 9-10), passives (scores 7-8), and detractors (scores 0-6). Calculating the NPS by minusing the percentage of detractors from the percentage of promoters empowers product managers in the video game industry with a clear and quantifiable understanding of player sentiment and loyalty, vital for nurturing a successful gaming product.

The significance of NPS in the video game realm is profound. A high NPS reflects a vibrant community of engaged players, eager to share their enthusiasm, fostering organic growth and expanded user acquisition. In contrast, a low NPS signals areas of concern, spurring vital investigations into player feedback and game mechanics. This feedback loop catalyzes continuous improvement, ensuring that games not only meet but transcend player expectations. In the competitive landscape of video games, a strong NPS stands out, making a product more appealing to both players and potential partners.

Delving into player feedback is crucial for elevating NPS. Product managers must look beyond the aggregate score to unearth the underlying reasons for both positive and negative sentiments. Utilizing qualitative and quantitative analysis methods allows managers to spot recurring themes in player experiences—ranging from game mechanics and graphics to storylines and customer support. Such insights inform targeted improvements that resonate deeply with the player base. By integrating player feedback into the development cycle, the product is enhanced while fostering a sense of community, with players feeling their voices are not just heard but valued.

In-game rewards and loyalty programs are

essential in uplifting NPS. A well-structured rewards system motivates players to engage more profoundly with the game, amplifying their chances of becoming promoters. Recognizing and rewarding player loyalty cultivates a positive feedback loop, where players feel inspired to promote the game within their networks. This approach not only elevates NPS but also strengthens player retention, for individuals are more inclined to invest in a game that appreciates and acknowledges their commitment.

Gamifying the feedback process can unlock even greater player engagement with NPS initiatives. Transforming feedback collection into an interactive and rewarding journey can raise participation rates and yield richer data. By infusing surveys with game-like mechanics, offering rewards for feedback contributions, and enabling social sharing, players' perceptions of the feedback process can shift dramatically. Additionally, influencer partnerships and innovative marketing campaigns can extend the reach of NPS messaging, inviting new players while simultaneously emphasizing the essence of community feedback. Through these strategies, product managers can cultivate a thriving ecosystem that perpetually enhances both NPS and the overall player experience.

Measuring NPS in the Gaming Industry

Net Promoter Score (NPS) serves as a powerful beacon to measure customer loyalty and satisfaction, focusing on the pivotal question: how likely are you to recommend a product or service to others? This insightful metric categorizes responses on a scale of 0 to 10 into three groups: promoters (scores 9-10), passives (scores 7-8), and detractors (scores 0-6). Calculating the NPS by minusing the percentage of detractors from the percentage of promoters empowers product managers in the video game industry with a clear and quantifiable understanding of player sentiment and loyalty, vital for nurturing a successful gaming product.

The significance of NPS in the video

game realm is profound. A high NPS reflects a vibrant community of engaged players, eager to share their enthusiasm, fostering organic growth and expanded user acquisition. In contrast, a low NPS signals areas of concern, spurring vital investigations into player feedback and game mechanics. This feedback loop catalyzes continuous improvement, ensuring that games not only meet but transcend player expectations. In the competitive landscape of video games, a strong NPS stands out, making a product more appealing to both players and potential partners.

Delving into player feedback is crucial for elevating NPS. Product managers must look beyond the aggregate score to unearth the underlying reasons for both positive and negative sentiments. Utilizing qualitative and quantitative analysis methods allows managers to spot recurring themes in player experiences—ranging from game mechanics and graphics to storylines and customer support. Such insights inform targeted improvements that resonate deeply with the player base. By integrating player feedback into the development cycle, the product is enhanced while fostering a sense of community, with players feeling their voices are not just heard but valued.

In-game rewards and loyalty programs are essential in uplifting NPS. A well-structured rewards system motivates players to engage more profoundly with the game, amplifying their chances of becoming promoters. Recognizing and rewarding player loyalty cultivates a positive feedback loop, where players feel inspired to promote the game within their networks. This approach not only elevates NPS but also strengthens player retention, for individuals are more inclined to invest in a game that appreciates and acknowledges their commitment.

Gamifying the feedback process can unlock even greater player engagement with NPS initiatives. Transforming feedback collection into an interactive and rewarding journey can raise participation rates and yield richer data. By infusing surveys with game-like mechanics, offering rewards for feedback contributions, and enabling social sharing, players' perceptions of the feedback process can shift dramatically. Additionally, influencer partnerships and innovative marketing campaigns can extend the reach of NPS messaging, inviting new players while simultaneously emphasizing the essence of community feedback. Through these strategies, product managers can cultivate a thriving ecosystem that perpetually enhances both NPS and the overall player experience.

Interpreting NPS Results

Interpreting Net Promoter Score (NPS) results is a vital opportunity for product managers in the gaming industry to elevate player experience and retention. NPS serves as a powerful metric that categorizes players into three groups: promoters, passives, and detractors. By understanding the distribution of these groups, product managers can gain valuable insights into player sentiment and loyalty. Analyzing the balance of promoters, who enthusiastically recommend the game, against detractors, who may dissuade others, is the essential first step towards crafting targeted strategies that enhance player satisfaction and elevate the NPS.

Once players have been categorized, diving deeper into the motivations behind their ratings becomes key. Engaging in qualitative research through player feedback and surveys can uncover the specific features or experiences that resonate most with promoters, alongside the challenges faced by detractors. Aspects such as gameplay mechanics, storytelling, graphics, and community involvement often emerge as significant influences on player opinions. By systematically analyzing this feedback, product managers can pinpoint actionable improvements, focusing on initiatives that promise to make the most impactful change to NPS.

In-game rewards and loyalty programs are powerful tools that can greatly enhance player satisfaction and, in turn, NPS. Implementing tiered rewards systems creates exciting incentives for continued play and engagement. By tuning into the preferences of promoters, product managers can design rewards that amplify their gaming experience, cultivating a deeper bond with the game. Loyalty programs appreciating long-term players can foster a profound sense of belonging, reinforcing their role as advocates who are poised to champion the game.

Gamifying the feedback process can also be transformative in interpreting and improving NPS results. By embedding fun and engaging methods for players to share their thoughts, product managers can inspire greater player participation. Techniques such as interactive surveys, in-game polls, or feedback forums that reward engagement enable richer insights into player sentiment and preferences, empowering product managers to tailor their strategies with precision.

Finally, harnessing influencer partnerships and dynamic marketing campaigns can magnify the effect of positive NPS results. Collaborating with influencers who connect with the target audience creates an opportunity for authentic word-of-mouth and the attraction of new players. By analyzing the relationship between influencer-driven initiatives and shifts in NPS and player engagement, product managers can align their marketing strategies with player feedback. This synergy creates compelling narratives that not only enhance the game's reputation but also inspire both current and potential players to become dedicated promoters.

Collecting Player Feedback Effectively

Collecting player feedback effectively is a vital step toward elevating your game's Net Promoter Score (NPS) and nurturing a thriving community. Understanding player sentiment and preferences can illuminate the path for your product development and marketing strategies. By implementing a structured feedback collection process with diverse methods, such as surveys, in-game prompts, and community forums, you can capture invaluable insights. Embracing various channels will deepen your understanding of player experiences and expectations.

In-game surveys strategically placed at key moments, like after completing a level or defeating a boss or achieving a milestone, are powerful tools for gathering feedback. Keep these surveys concise, focusing on gameplay mechanics, difficulty levels, and overall satisfaction. Adding gamification elements can transform these surveys into engaging experiences, encouraging participation and rewarding players for their valuable input.

Harnessing the power of the internet and social media and community forums fosters a vibrant platform for player expression. By monitoring discussions on Reddit, Discord, and Twitter, you can gain real-time feedback and identify emerging trends. Engaging directly with players builds a sense of community and loyalty, illustrating that their voices matter. This interaction unearths qualitative insights that traditional methods might overlook, enriching your understanding further. After collecting feedback, effectively analyzing the data is crucial for informed decision-making. Utilizing data analysis tools allows you to spot patterns and trends, enabling you to prioritize improvements. Categorizing feedback into actionable insights streamlines the implementation process and enhances communication with stakeholders and team members.

Finally, closing the feedback loop is essential for fostering trust and engagement among players. After implementing changes based on their input, communicate these updates to the community. Showcasing how player feedback has shaped game design nurtures loyalty and encourages ongoing participation in feedback processes. By cultivating a cycle of collecting, analyzing, implementing, and communicating feedback, you can forge a dynamic relationship with your player base, paving the way for an improved NPS and the success of your game.

Tools for Feedback Analysis

In the exciting world of video game development, the power of player feedback serves as a beacon for enhancing the Net Promoter Score (NPS). A myriad of tools emerges to empower product managers in their quest to extract actionable insights from player input. These range from straightforward survey platforms to advanced analytics software capable of deciphering vast amounts of data. By harnessing these tools, product managers unveil trends in player sentiment, measure satisfaction, and discover opportunities for growth, ultimately igniting engagement and loyalty.

Survey platforms like SurveyMonkey and Typeform offer an inviting gateway to gather feedback straight from players. With these tools, product managers can craft custom surveys that delve into specific facets of the game, such as gameplay mechanics, graphics, or in-game rewards. Thoughtful survey design captures both quantitative data through rating scales and qualitative insights through open-ended questions. This valuable feedback illuminates strengths and weaknesses, guiding informed decisions that resonate with player desires.

Beyond traditional survey methods, advanced analytics platforms such as Google Analytics and Mixpanel deliver profound insights into player behavior. These tools empower product managers to track key engagement metrics like session duration, retention rates, and in-game purchases. By correlating these insights with survey feedback, product managers cultivate a holistic understanding of how game features shape player satisfaction. This data-driven focus prioritizes development efforts that elevate the player experience and enhance the NPS.

Incorporating gamification into the feedback process can spark higher engagement rates. Tools like Qualaroo and UserVoice bring gamified elements to feedback collection, transforming it into an enjoyable experience for players. Rewarding feedback contributions with in-game rewards or loyalty points not only boosts participation but also fosters positive associations with the brand. This innovative approach nurtures a culture of open dialogue between developers and the player community, enriching the overall gaming experience.

Finally, forging partnerships with influencers amplifies feedback analysis efforts. Tools that enable social listening—like Brandwatch or Hootsuite—allow product managers to tune into conversations about their game across social media platforms. By grasping the sentiments shared by influencers and the wider gaming community, product managers can recalibrate their strategies to resonate more closely with player expectations. Collaborating with influencers to champion feedback initiatives can further elevate engagement. As product managers embrace these tools for feedback analysis, they embark on a journey to master the intricate landscape of player satisfaction and cultivate a passionate gaming community.

Identifying Key Themes and Trends

Identifying key themes and trends in the realm of video games is essential for product managers dedicated to enhancing their game's Net Promoter Score (NPS). A thorough analysis of player feedback unveils profound insights into what players truly value. By categorizing and prioritizing this feedback, product managers can discover recurring themes that resonate across the player base, such as game mechanics, user interface design, narrative depth, and community engagement. Recognizing these trends opens the door to targeted improvements that lead to increased player satisfaction and loyalty. One of the most powerful methods to gather player feedback is through structured surveys, carefully crafted to elicit specific responses related to in-game experiences, features, and overall enjoyment. Analyzing this feedback reveals areas where players feel engaged or frustrated. Furthermore, leveraging qualitative insights from forums, social media, and in-game chat uncovers emerging trends that structured surveys might overlook. By triangulating data from diverse sources, product managers can form a vivid picture of player sentiment, highlighting key themes that deserve attention.

In-game rewards and loyalty programs stand at the forefront of enhancing player engagement and loyalty. Trends reveal that players are more inclined to promote a game when they feel recognized and rewarded for their dedication. Implementing tiered rewards systems or offering exclusive content to long-term players cultivates a sense of belonging and investment in the game. Moreover, understanding which types of rewards resonate most with players— whether cosmetic items, gameplay advantages, or community recognition— can inspire the design of more impactful loyalty programs.

Gamifying the feedback process itself is an exciting trend that product managers can harness to boost player participation in feedback initiatives. By weaving game-like elements into feedback mechanisms, such as leaderboards, badges, or progress tracking, players may feel more motivated to share their thoughts. This approach not only amplifies the volume of feedback but also enriches the quality of insights gathered, as players become more engaged in the process. Identifying the right gamification strategies can transform feedback into an inspiring experience.

Influencer partnerships and marketing campaigns offer yet another powerful avenue for recognizing and amplifying key themes and trends. Collaborating with gamers and influencers who resonate with the target demographic brings unique insights into player expectations and preferences. Influencers act as a bridge between developers and players, delivering invaluable feedback that highlights emerging trends in player behavior. By analyzing the content created by influencers, product managers can uncover what excites players and what themes are poised to take off, enabling more informed choices in game development and marketing strategies.

Prioritizing Player Feedback

Prioritizing player feedback is vital for elevating the Net Promoter Score (NPS) of any video game. Understanding what players cherish and what detracts from their journey empowers product managers to make impactful decisions that resonate deeply with their audience. By systematically gathering, analyzing, and implementing player feedback, developers can nurture a loyal player base that feels valued and heard. This transformative process not only fuels enhancements in game design but also creates an atmosphere where players are excited to recommend the game to others, ultimately boosting NPS.

To effectively harness player feedback, product managers should embrace a diverse array of channels. While traditional surveys and questionnaires are useful, they can be enriched with dynamic methods such as in-game feedback prompts, community forums, and social media engagement. These avenues facilitate real-time feedback and illuminate trends and areas for growth. Additionally, utilizing analytics tools can offer profound insights into player behavior, enabling product managers to uncover specific pain points or moments of joy within the gaming experience.

Once feedback is captured, the next step is prioritization. Recognizing that not all feedback carries the same significance, categorizing it based on frequency, severity, and potential impact on player satisfaction is essential. Product managers should concentrate on feedback that influences a large segment of the player base or aligns with the game's core objectives. Furthermore, leveraging A/B testing can reveal which changes resonate most positively with players, fostering data-driven decisions that empower and uplift the community.

Implementing player feedback can be further enriched through in-game rewards and loyalty programs. By acknowledging players for their insights, developers not only enhance engagement but also cultivate a culture of participation and investment among the community. Offering exclusive in-game items, currency, or access to new features in exchange for feedback can inspire players to share their thoughts. This approach not only elevates the player experience but significantly increases the chances of players becoming passionate advocates for the game, thereby enhancing NPS.

Finally, collaborating with influencers and integrating marketing campaigns can amplify the significance of player feedback. Influencers often have direct connections to player communities and can effectively communicate the value of providing feedback. By spotlighting player-driven changes in marketing materials, product managers can demonstrate their unwavering commitment to player satisfaction, reinforcing the message that player opinions truly matter. This strategy not only builds player trust but also positions the game as one that genuinely values its community, propelling an increase in Net Promoter Score.

Developing Actionable Insights

Developing actionable insights is essential for product managers striving to elevate the Net Promoter Score (NPS) for video games. By diving deep into player feedback, product managers can uncover patterns and trends that illuminate what players truly cherish in their gaming journey. This transformative process begins with gathering data from diverse sources, including in-game surveys, social media platforms, and vibrant player forums. Harnessing both qualitative and quantitative methods ensures a rich understanding of player sentiment. The objective is to navigate this feedback landscape to extract important insights that can guide product development and marketing endeavors.

After gathering this invaluable feedback, the next step is to categorize and prioritize insights based on their potential impact on the NPS. Product managers should group feedback into key themes, such as gameplay mechanics, story elements, and in-game rewards. This strategic categorization empowers teams to focus on the most critical areas that can enhance player satisfaction and loyalty. Techniques like affinity mapping can illuminate connections between various pieces of feedback, simplifying the identification of common concerns or desires among players.

Implementing strategies that respond directly to player feedback is vital for closing the loop and showcasing the value of player input. Product managers should create action plans that detail specific initiatives aimed at addressing insights derived from player feedback. For example, if players express a desire for more diverse in-game rewards, teams can prioritize the creation of new reward structures or loyalty programs. By outlining clear timelines and responsibilities for implementation, product managers can turn these insights into tangible game enhancements, ultimately leading to a higher NPS.

Incorporating gamification into the feedback process can elevate player engagement and loyalty. By designing feedback mechanisms that reward players for their contributions, product managers can cultivate a more interactive and enjoyable experience. Implementing a system where players earn in-game currency or exclusive items for completing surveys can inspire participation. This not only amplifies the volume of feedback collected but also fosters a sense of community and investment among players, motivating them to advocate for the game within their circles.

Finally, forming partnerships with influencers and leveraging marketing campaigns can magnify the impact of actionable insights derived from player feedback. Collaborating with influencers who resonate with the game's target audience can spread the word about the positive experiences and improvements resulting from player suggestions. Additionally, marketing initiatives that celebrate changes made in response to player feedback can strengthen the bond between players and the game. This proactive approach does not just enhance player satisfaction; it enriches the brand perception, ultimately paving the way for a higher NPS.

Communicating Changes to Players

Communicating changes to players is a

vital element of nurturing a strong bond between game developers and the gaming community. Effective communication empowers players by keeping them informed of updates, clarifying the rationale behind changes, and making them feel valued in the decision-making journey. This transparency builds trust and enhances loyalty, significantly impacting the Net Promoter Score (NPS). Product managers have the opportunity to craft messages that resonate deeply with their audience, addressing concerns and highlighting the positive aspects of the changes.

One powerful strategy involves harnessing multiple channels to connect with players. Utilizing social media platforms, in-game notifications, and community forums creates diverse pathways for sharing important updates. Each channel reaches a unique audience, and customizing messages can ignite engagement. A quick announcement on Twitter captures immediate attention, while an in-depth blog post provides meaningful insights, enriching players' understanding of the changes and their significance. By engaging players through various communication methods, product managers can deliver consistent messages that showcase the value of updates. Timing the communication effectively is equally crucial. Announcing changes during peak player engagement moments ensures heightened visibility and interaction. By analyzing player activity data, product managers can identify these prime times. Moreover, proactive communication before implementing changes prepares players mentally, fostering acceptance and appreciation of modifications. When players feel involved and informed about the upcoming changes, they embrace the journey positively.

The tone and language of messages profoundly influence communication's impact. Avoiding technical jargon fosters inclusivity, allowing all players to connect with the dialogue. Clear and relatable language builds a bridge to understanding, while incorporating player feedback directly into messaging demonstrates genuine appreciation for their perspectives. Acknowledging specific concerns and explaining how changes address these issues cultivates a sense of community and shared purpose.

Finally, following up after changes are implemented is essential. Gathering player feedback on modifications offers invaluable insights into their reception and effectiveness. Encouraging players to express their thoughts through surveys, forums, or direct channels reinforces the notion that their input shapes the development process. This ongoing dialogue not only refines future updates but also cements the idea that players are at the heart of the journey. When players feel heard and valued, they are inspired to champion the game to others, leaving a lasting impact on NPS.

Designing Effective Reward Systems

Designing effective reward systems is a powerful way to enhance player engagement and elevate Net Promoter Scores (NPS) in video games. A thoughtfully crafted reward system not only inspires players to participate actively but also motivates them to share meaningful feedback. By understanding the deep motivations of your player base, product managers can unlock the secrets of what players truly value. This understanding paves the way for rewards that resonate with players, nurturing loyalty and boosting overall satisfaction.

In-game rewards can take on many forms, from virtual currency and exclusive items to cosmetic enhancements. Each type of reward serves an original purpose and they should appeal to different segments of the player demographic. Competitive players are often driven by rewards that enhance gameplay, while casual players may cherish cosmetic items that reflect their individuality. By segmenting the player base and tailoring rewards accordingly, product managers can craft a more personalized experience that ignites player engagement and inspires advocacy for the game.

Implementing loyalty programs represents another compelling strategy to enhance player retention and satisfaction. These programs celebrate players for their ongoing engagement, whether it's completing daily challenges, participating in events, or reaching significant milestones. The introduction of tiered rewards can further motivate players to remain active over time. As players climb through loyalty tiers, they unlock increasingly valuable rewards, fostering a sense of achievement and encouraging continued participation. This gamification of reward systems not only strengthens player retention but also cultivates a community of devoted advocates who are eager to recommend the game to others. Integrating feedback processes into the reward system can profoundly enrich the player experience. By gamifying feedback collection, product managers transform player insights into a rewarding activity. Players can earn rewards for completing surveys, participating in focus groups, or sharing thoughts on new features. This approach increases both the quantity and quality of feedback while making players feel valued and integral to the game's evolution. By recognizing their contributions and rewarding their input, developers can forge a deeper connection between the player community and the game.

Lastly, influencer partnerships and marketing campaigns can amplify the power of reward systems. Collaborating with influencers who speak to your audience creates excitement around new rewards, driving player interest and engagement. Influencers can illuminate the benefits of loyalty programs and showcase exclusive in-game rewards, effectively reaching a broader audience. By integrating influencer marketing into the reward strategy, product managers can elevate visibility and create a sense of aspiration among players, further igniting engagement and loyalty.

The Role of Loyalty Programs in NPS

Loyalty programs have become a vital force in elevating the Net Promoter Score (NPS) for video games. These programs reward players for their ongoing engagement while cultivating a sense of community and belonging. By offering tangible incentives that encourage active participation, loyalty programs can profoundly enhance player satisfaction and advocacy. Embracing the mechanics of effective loyalty programs empowers product managers to craft strategies that resonate deeply with their audience and drive higher NPS.

One of the remarkable advantages of loyalty programs lies in their capacity to collect invaluable player feedback. By integrating feedback mechanisms such as surveys or in-game polls, product managers can directly capture insights about player preferences and experiences. This feedback loop is critical for endless improvement, enabling teams to make data-driven decisions that elevate gameplay and overall satisfaction. When players feel their voices are acknowledged and their suggestions are embraced, they are more likely to recommend the game to others, thus boosting NPS.

In-game rewards linked to loyalty programs can further enhance player engagement and retention. Offering exclusive items, advance access to new content, or special events for dedicated players not only incentivizes continued play but also fosters a sense of achievement and exclusivity. These rewards can be gamified, tapping into players' competitive spirit and inspiring them to engage more actively in the community. When players experience the tangible benefits of their loyalty, they are more inclined to share their positive experiences with others, amplifying their role as passionate promoters of the game.

Implementing a successful loyalty program requires thoughtful design and structure. Product managers should strive to create a seamless experience that integrates effortlessly with the game's existing systems. This entails ensuring that the reward system is clear and that players understand how to earn and redeem their rewards. Moreover, leveraging data analytics to tailor the program to player behaviors and preferences can lead to more personalized experiences, enhancing the likelihood of positive feedback and higher NPS.

Finally, partnerships with influencers can significantly amplify the impact of loyalty programs. Collaborating with respected figures in the gaming community allows product managers to showcase the loyalty program to a broader audience, highlighting its benefits and enticing new players to join. Influencers can offer authentic testimonials and highlight the rewards, enhancing the program's appeal. This approach not only boosts visibility but also reinforces credibility, as players are more inclined to trust recommendations from admired personalities. Consequently, a well-executed loyalty program, bolstered by influencer marketing, can become a powerful catalyst for driving NPS in the world of video games.

Case Studies of Successful Programs

In the realm of video games, various companies have embarked on a journey to enhance their Net Promoter Score (NPS) by prioritizing player feedback and engagement. A remarkable example is the popular multiplayer game that integrated a robust player feedback system directly into its user interface. By empowering players to share their thoughts and experiences in real-time, the developers unlocked actionable insights. This initiative not only enriched the game's features but also nurtured a vibrant community among players, leading to a remarkable increase in their NPS.

Another inspiring case study involves a leading gaming studio that launched an all-encompassing loyalty program. This initiative honored players for their engagement and commitment over time, offering in-game currency, exclusive items, and access to special events. By gamifying the feedback process, the developers created a scenario where rewards were linked to player surveys and interactions. As players felt appreciated for their contributions, they were more inclined to recommend the game to others. The loyalty program fostered a harmonious relationship that propelled the NPS upward, benefiting both players and developers alike.

A third example showcases a strategic partnership between a game developer and influential figures in the gaming community. Through collaboration with these influencers, the company reached wider audiences while gathering authentic feedback on gameplay experiences. The influencers engaged with audiences live, sharing their honest opinions and prompting followers to participate in feedback processes. This approach refined the game based on genuine player insights and increased visibility, resulting in heightened player acquisition and retention. The outcome was a significant rise in NPS, fueled by the meaningful connections forged through influencer marketing.

Moreover, a mobile game developer acknowledged the value of continuous player engagement through seasonal content updates. By creating a feedback loop where players could suggest themes for upcoming events, the developers instilled a sense of ownership among their players. This endeavor facilitated the delivery of tailored content that resonated deeply with the player base, increasing satisfaction and loyalty. Utilizing gamification techniques, such as progress tracking and achievement badges, encouraged active participation in feedback initiatives. This enriched the gaming experience and contributed to a measurable increase in NPS.

Lastly, a notable success story emerged from a game that harnessed data analytics to assess player behavior and preferences. By analyzing player interactions and feedback, the developers pinpointed essential areas for improvement. They made targeted changes, adjusting game difficulty levels and enhancing user experience based on player demographics. Coupled with effective communication strategies that transparently illustrated how player feedback influenced changes, trust and loyalty among players flourished. This data-driven approach significantly elevated the NPS, showcasing the transformative power of informed decision-making within the gaming industry.

Principles of Gamification

Gamification harnesses the power of game mechanics and design elements in non-game contexts to elevate user engagement and motivation. For product managers, grasping the principles of gamification is vital for boosting a video game's Net Promoter Score (NPS). By weaving in elements such as points, badges, and leaderboards, product managers can craft a more immersive experience that ignites players' passion and commitment to the game. This approach not only draws in new players but also strengthens retention among existing users, leading to an enhanced NPS.

Central to the concept of gamification is intrinsic motivation—the drive to engage in an activity for the joy it brings. When players experience achievement and progress, they are more inclined to continue their journey and share their enthusiasm with others.

Product managers should design challenges that strike the perfect balance; if too easy, players may lose interest, but if too hard, they could feel frustration. By employing a tiered difficulty system or adaptive challenges that adjust to player skill levels, managers can sustain a high level of engagement, inspiring players to offer positive feedback and heartfelt recommendations.

Another cornerstone principle is the implementation of feedback loops. Effective gamification integrates mechanisms that provide players with immediate feedback on their actions, reinforcing desired behaviors and fostering deeper engagement. For instance, in-game notifications or visual cues showcasing progress or achievements can keep players informed and motivated. Furthermore, incorporating player feedback mechanisms directly into the game enriches the overall experience, allowing players to feel valued. This sense of transparency can dramatically elevate player loyalty and advocacy.

In-game rewards and loyalty programs

represent yet another critical facet of gamification. Product managers should thoughtfully structure rewards to not only celebrate player achievements but also promote ongoing interaction with the game. This could encompass exclusive content, special items, or recognition within the community. By establishing a tiered loyalty system that offers increasingly valuable rewards, managers can motivate players to engage more frequently and share their experiences, enhancing the game's visibility and allure.

Lastly, influencer partnerships and marketing campaigns can thrive on gamification principles by crafting interactive experiences that resonate with target audiences. Collaborating with influencers to design challenges or competitions can fuel engagement and encourage players to actively participate. By tapping into social media platforms for these campaigns, product managers can cultivate a sense of community and belonging among players, which translates into higher NPS. Combining captivating content with community-driven initiatives not only enriches player satisfaction but also nurtures advocates who are eager to recommend the game to their networks.

Implementing Gamification in Feedback Collection

Implementing gamification in feedback collection can truly transform player engagement and elevate the quality of insights gathered from users. By infusing game-like elements into the feedback process, product managers can turn mundane surveys into interactive experiences that resonate deeply with players. This innovative approach not only incentivizes participation but also fosters thoughtful responses, ultimately leading to a richer understanding of player sentiment. Incorporating elements such as points, leaderboards, and achievement badges cultivates a sense of competition and accomplishment, driving higher response rates and generating more vibrant data.

To effectively harness the power of gamification, it's vital to design feedback mechanisms that align with players' intrinsic motivations and preferences. Understanding the target audience is key; product managers should delve into player demographics and behavior patterns to tailor gamified elements for maximum impact. For instance, younger players may respond enthusiastically to mobile-based feedback systems that offer immediate rewards, while veteran players might cherish challenges that acknowledge their long-term dedication to the game. By customizing the feedback experience, product managers can create an atmosphere where players feel genuinely valued and are more inclined to share their insights.

In-game rewards serve as a compelling motivator for players to engage in feedback collection. Offering tangible benefits—like exclusive in-game items, currency, or access to new content—can significantly amplify participation rates. Product managers can design specific feedback quests that inspire players to complete designated tasks in exchange for rewards. This strategy not only invites feedback but also enriches the overall gaming experience, as players feel they are actively contributing to the game's development while enjoying meaningful perks. A tiered reward system can enhance this engagement further, providing escalating incentives based on the frequency or quality of feedback offered.

Collaborating with influencers can magnify the reach and effectiveness of gamified feedback initiatives. Influencers possess established connections with their audiences, making them ideal allies in promoting feedback campaigns. By leveraging their platforms, product managers can inspire players to participate in feedback activities, emphasizing the fun and rewarding nature of the process. Influencers can speak to and share their own experiences with the feedback collection, showcasing the benefits of participation and sparking increased engagement among their followers, broadening the response base.

Finally, tracking and analyzing the data collected through gamified feedback mechanisms is crucial for ongoing improvement. Product managers should establish clear metrics to assess the effectiveness of their gamification strategies, considering aspects such as response rates, completion times, and the quality of feedback received. By regularly reviewing these metrics, product managers can identify trends and areas for enhancement, facilitating iterative improvements to the feedback process. Embracing a data-driven outlook ensures that gamification not only elevates engagement but also leads to actionable insights that profoundly impact game development and player satisfaction.

Measuring the Impact of Gamification on NPS

Measuring the impact of gamification on Net Promoter Score (NPS) is an inspiring journey that aligns player engagement strategies with user feedback mechanisms. To embark on this transformative assessment, product managers must define what successful gamification truly looks like through clear metrics. Key performance indicators such as player retention rates, frequency of engagement with gamified elements, and overall satisfaction ratings serve as essential data points. By correlating these metrics with NPS, product managers can uncover how gamification initiatives spark players' enthusiasm to recommend the game to others.

The implementation of in-game rewards and loyalty programs stands as a pivotal aspect of gamification that significantly uplifts NPS. Rewards systems not only enhance the player's experience but also inspire users to share their feedback. By analyzing insights from players who engage with reward systems, product managers can identify trends and preferences, refining the rewards and gameplay. This ongoing process boosts player satisfaction and directly links gamification to an increased willingness for players to promote the game to their peers.

Moreover, gamifying feedback processes revolutionizes how players connect with the game's development team. By integrating feedback mechanisms within the game, such as mini-surveys or interactive polls that reward participation, product managers gather valuable data while enriching the player experience. This engaging approach signals to players that their opinions matter, fostering increased loyalty and a higher NPS.

Influencer partnerships and marketing campaigns play a vital role in harnessing gamification to elevate NPS. Collaborating with influencers who resonate with the gaming community magnifies the impact of gamified features and rewards programs. When influencers actively engage in these initiatives, they draw attention and lend credibility, creating a ripple effect of enthusiasm. By tracking NPS changes after these campaigns, product managers can gauge the success of influencer-driven gamification strategies and adapt their methods to inspire even greater connections.

In essence, measuring the impact of gamification on NPS embodies a multifaceted strategy that harmonizes quantitative metrics with qualitative player feedback. By embracing in-game rewards, enhancing feedback processes, and leveraging influencer partnerships, product managers can cultivate a holistic approach to gamification that enriches the player experience and drives higher NPS. Continuous analysis of these elements empowers teams to adapt and refine their strategies, meeting the evolving expectations of their player base and fostering a community of loyal advocates.

Identifying the Right Influencers

Identifying the correct influencers is an important step in elevating your game's Net Promoter Score (NPS). As product managers, it is vital to understand that not all influencers carry the same weight. The perfect influencer should resonate deeply with your target audience and embody your brand values. Start by envisioning the specific traits of your ideal influencer, such as follower demographics, engagement rates, and the type of content they create.

This clarity will empower you to make choices that can significantly enhance your game's reputation and player involvement.

Harness the power of data analytics tools to thoroughly assess potential influencers. Look beyond mere follower counts; delve into engagement metrics like likes, shares, and comments. An influencer with a smaller yet passionate audience can be far more impactful than one boasting a large but disengaged following. Additionally, evaluate the influencer's past partnerships and their relevance to your game's genre and themes. This analysis will ensure their audience is genuinely interested, increasing the likelihood of positive player experiences.

The authenticity of the influencers you consider is equally crucial. Today's consumers are wise and can easily identify inauthentic endorsements. Investigate the influencer's content history and audience interactions to determine their credibility and trustworthiness. Partnering with influencers who have fostered genuine connections can spark more effective marketing campaigns and nurture loyalty among players, ultimately driving a higher NPS.

Effective collaboration with the right influencers requires transparent communication of your goals. Whether your aim is to promote a new game feature, launch a loyalty program, or gather insightful feedback, ensure that the influencer grasps your objectives. Work together on content creation that authentically showcases your game while allowing the influencer to retain their unique voice. This harmony can craft a compelling narrative that resonates with their audience and inspires player engagement.

Lastly, closely monitor the impact of influencer partnerships on your game's NPS. Establish metrics to evaluate the success of these collaborations, centering on player feedback, engagement levels, and retention rates. This data will illuminate the effectiveness of current campaigns and offer invaluable insights for future influencer strategies. By continuously refining your approach and adapting to player needs, you can cultivate a devoted player base and elevate your game's overall NPS.

Building Successful Partnerships

Building successful partnerships is vital for product managers looking to elevate the Net Promoter Score (NPS) of their video games. Collaborating with influencers, developers, and community leaders can transform player engagement and satisfaction. By nurturing strong relationships, product managers can harness the expertise and reach of their partners, crafting a richer and more rewarding experience for players. These partnerships must align with the brand's core values and objectives, ensuring mutual benefit and a collective focus on enhancing player loyalty and satisfaction.

A crucial element of creating successful partnerships lies in understanding the needs and preferences of both players and partners. Conducting thorough player feedback analysis unlocks insights into what captivates the audience. This insight affords for the identification of potential partners who share a similar target demographic or brand ethos. Engaging these partners through joint ventures or co-marketing initiatives can magnify promotional efforts while cultivating a vibrant community of players.

In-game rewards and loyalty programs offer exciting avenues for collaboration. By teaming up with external brands or influencers, product managers can design exclusive rewards that incentivize player engagement and feedback. Incorporating unique in-game items or experiences linked to a partner's brand can spark participation in feedback initiatives while enhancing the game's allure. This strategy not only strengthens player loyalty but also empowers players to champion the game within their networks, amplifying positive NPS outcomes.

The gamification of feedback processes can thrive through strategic partnerships. Collaborating with experts in game design or feedback methodologies opens the door to innovative approaches that elevate the feedback experience for players. By weaving game mechanics into feedback collection—like progress tracking or competitive elements—product managers can boost participation rates, ensuring that the insights gathered are both meaningful and actionable. This approach enriches the player experience and fosters a culture of continuous improvement within game development.

Finally, influencer partnerships can be a powerful catalyst for marketing campaigns aimed at boosting NPS. Influencers who authentically connect with the gaming community can deliver genuine endorsements that ignite player engagement and feedback. By choosing influencers who resonate with the game's values and target audience, product managers can design impactful campaigns that drive awareness and nurture loyalty. These partnerships should be cultivated over time, with ongoing communication and collaboration, ensuring that influencers remain engaged and aligned with the game's evolving narrative. Ultimately, successful partnerships can create a thriving ecosystem that champions ongoing player engagement and satisfaction.

Leveraging Influencer Feedback for NPS

Harnessing influencer feedback to elevate Net Promoter Score (NPS) is a visionary strategy that empowers product managers in the gaming industry to truly connect with player sentiments and enrich their games. Influencers occupy a pivotal role in the gaming ecosystem, acting as essential conduits between developers and the passionate gaming community. Their insights are invaluable, shedding light on player preferences, satisfaction, and areas ripe for improvement. By weaving influencer feedback into the NPS framework, product managers can unlock a deeper understanding of player experiences and aspirations.

The journey begins with forging partnerships with key figures in the gaming community—identifying influencers whose audiences resonate with the game's target demographic. Once these relationships are established, product managers can invite influencers to explore new features, share feedback, and recount their experiences with their followers. This collaboration not only enhances credibility but also amplifies player voices, illuminating a broader spectrum of player sentiments that significantly influence NPS.

To effectively incorporate influencer feedback into player feedback analysis, a systematic approach is essential. Product managers should create dedicated channels for influencers to share their insights, such as surveys, interviews, or feedback sessions after gameplay. Analyzing this data alongside traditional player feedback enables the identification of trends and correlations. By juxtaposing influencer insights with NPS data, product managers can reveal specific areas for enhancement and validate changes that resonate with the wider player base.

Moreover, influencers are vital in promoting in-game rewards and loyalty programs, which are key drivers of player satisfaction and loyalty. By sharing their positive experiences with these initiatives, influencers can inspire their followers to engage more deeply with the game, fostering an improvement in NPS. Product managers should seize the opportunity to collaborate with influencers in co-creating these programs, ensuring alignment with player desires and an overall enriched gaming experience.

Lastly, gamifying the feedback process can amplify the impact of influencer insights. By introducing challenges or competitions that motivate influencers to share their insights in engaging and innovative ways, product managers can cultivate a dynamic and entertaining feedback loop. This approach not only invigorates influencers but also sparks enthusiasm among their followers, driving higher engagement and improving NPS. By thoughtfully integrating influencer feedback into their strategies, product managers can inspire remarkable advancements in game performance and player satisfaction.

Creating Engaging Marketing Strategies

Crafting engaging marketing strategies is essential for product managers striving to elevate the Net Promoter Score (NPS) of their video games. A powerful marketing strategy centers on understanding player demographics, preferences, and behaviors. By harnessing data analytics, product managers can segment their audience and customize marketing initiatives. This focused approach not only amplifies the relevance of marketing messages but also builds a deeper connection with players, ultimately leading to heightened satisfaction and loyalty.

Player feedback analysis serves as a dynamic tool in developing impactful marketing strategies. By methodically gathering and analyzing feedback through surveys, social media, and in-game metrics, product managers can pinpoint areas for adjustment and opportunities for innovation. This feedback loop empowers teams to adapt their marketing efforts based on genuine player sentiments, ensuring that campaigns resonate with the audience. Furthermore, leveraging analytics tools allows product managers to track trends and shifts in player preferences, enabling proactive pivots in their strategies.

In-game rewards and loyalty programs are vital in crafting engaging marketing strategies. By integrating reward systems that recognize and incentivize player loyalty, product managers can boost player retention and satisfaction. Offering exclusive in-game items, early access to new content, or bonuses for referring friends transforms players into passionate advocates for the game. These loyalty programs also yield valuable insights into player behavior, informing future marketing campaigns and product development efforts.

Gamification of feedback processes is an innovative approach to engage players and refine marketing strategies. By infusing game-like elements into feedback collection, such as challenges, achievements, or leaderboards, product managers can inspire players to share their insights more actively. This enjoyable feedback process generates richer data for product teams while fostering a sense of community and ownership, enhancing the overall experience with the game.

Influencer partnerships and marketing campaigns serve to amplify the reach and impact of marketing strategies. Collaborating with gamers and influencers who resonate with the target audience allows product managers to tap into established communities and gain credibility. By crafting campaigns that align with influencer content, product managers create authentic promotional experiences that captivate players. Additionally, influencer feedback offers unique insights into player preferences and expectations, seamlessly integrating into ongoing marketing strategies to make sure they are relevant and effective.

Aligning Campaigns with Player Expectations

Aligning campaigns with player expectations is not just important; it's transformative for enhancing a game's Net Promoter Score (NPS). By truly understanding what players desire from their gaming experiences, product managers can craft campaigns that resonate deeply. This journey involves not only analyzing player feedback but also anticipating their future needs and preferences. When strategies align with players' expectations, a powerful connection is forged between the game and its audience, paving the way for heightened loyalty and satisfaction.

Player feedback analysis serves as the bedrock for this alignment. By harnessing both qualitative and quantitative data, product managers can uncover trends and gain insights into player sentiments. Surveys, in-game feedback mechanisms, and social media listening unveil what players cherish and what they seek to improve. Transforming this feedback into actionable strategies empowers product managers to address specific concerns or enhance desirable features, ensuring players feel heard and valued.

In-game rewards and loyalty programs emerge as dynamic tools in this alignment. Players yearn for recognition and tangible benefits for their engagement, and well-designed reward systems can fulfill this aspiration. By weaving player feedback into these programs, product managers can craft rewards that are meaningful and relevant. Customizing rewards to align with player preferences not only boosts satisfaction but also nurtures ongoing participation and advocacy, directly impacting NPS.

Gamification of feedback processes shines as an innovative strategy for aligning campaigns with player expectations. By making feedback engaging and rewarding, product managers can inspire players to share their thoughts and experiences. Infusing elements like points, badges, or leaderboards into the feedback experience fosters a sense of competition and community. This approach enhances feedback volume and encourages players to invest in the game's development, cultivating ownership and loyalty. Influencer partnerships and marketing campaigns also serve as powerful catalysts for alignment with player expectations. Collaborating with influencers who resonate with the target audience amplifies the message and ensures it mirrors what players value. By harnessing the authenticity of influencers, product managers can create campaigns perceived as genuine and relatable. This strategy not only drives awareness but also strengthens the bond between the game's offerings and player expectations, leading to higher satisfaction and improved NPS.

Measuring Campaign Success and NPS Impact

Measuring campaign success and the impact of Net Promoter Score (NPS) is vital for product managers striving to elevate their video game offerings. By quantifying the effectiveness of marketing strategies and player engagement initiatives, invaluable insights emerge. Establishing key performance indicators (KPIs) tied to NPS is essential for evaluating the direct outcomes of campaigns. Metrics such as player retention rates, engagement levels, and feedback volume shine a light on how effectively a campaign connects with its audience. Linking NPS scores to specific campaigns empowers product managers to uncover which strategies foster the highest levels of player satisfaction and loyalty.

To truly assess the impact of NPS, establishing a baseline score before launching new initiatives is fundamental. This baseline serves as a springboard for comparative analysis post-campaign, revealing shifts in player sentiment. Surveys conducted after significant updates, marketing campaigns, or in-game events offer immediate insights into player experiences. Analyzing these responses alongside NPS results uncovers specific factors driving player loyalty, adding depth to the understanding of influences behind positive or negative feedback.

Beyond direct player feedback, product managers should embrace the qualitative aspects of player experiences. Techniques like player interviews and focus groups illuminate deeper insights into player motivations and emotions towards the game. This qualitative data enriches quantitative NPS scores, creating a holistic view of player sentiment. Recognizing player pain points and areas of delight paves the way for future campaign strategies that resonate with players' needs and preferences.

In-game rewards and loyalty programs hold the power to transform NPS, making their measurement crucial. By tracking changes in NPS before and after launching these programs, product managers can evaluate their success in boosting player engagement. Segmentation analysis unveils how different player demographics react to varying rewards, enabling tailored approaches that maximize impact. Moreover, gamifying the feedback process through engaging surveys or interactive tools enhances participation rates and enriches the quality of insights gained.

Influencer partnerships and marketing campaigns offer remarkable opportunities to elevate NPS. Evaluating the success of these collaborations not only involves measuring immediate NPS changes but also analyzing their long-term effects on brand perception and player loyalty. Monitoring player acquisition rates and retention following influencer campaigns provides valuable insights into their effectiveness. By continuously examining the relationship between these marketing efforts and player satisfaction, product managers can refine their strategies, cultivating a devoted player base that actively champions the game's success.

Establishing a Feedback Loop

Establishing a feedback loop is essential for product managers striving to elevate the Net Promoter Score (NPS) of their video games. This process creates a pathway for continuous improvement fueled by player insights, fostering deeper engagement and unwavering loyalty. It all begins with collecting player feedback through diverse channels—such as in-game surveys, social media interactions, and user forums. By offering multiple avenues for feedback, product managers can capture a rich tapestry of opinions and experiences, providing priceless data for enhancing gameplay, features, and overall player satisfaction.

Once feedback is gathered, the next step is to dive into the data, unveiling key trends and opportunities for growth. Employing analytics tools can transform raw feedback into actionable insights. Product managers should focus on identifying patterns in player sentiments, especially regarding features that evoke both praise and criticism. Prioritizing these insights based on their potential impact on the player experience is vital. Concentrating on the most pressing concerns or suggestions allows product managers to allocate resources efficiently and tackle the issues that resonate most with their players.

Implementing changes based on player feedback marks the true embodiment of the feedback loop. After pinpointing vital areas for improvement, product managers should craft a clear action plan that addresses these insights.

This journey might involve refining game mechanics, introducing captivating new features, or enhancing in-game rewards and loyalty programs. Communicating these changes to players is crucial, as it solidifies the message that their feedback is cherished and taken to heart. Regular updates on how player suggestions shape the game fortify trust and nurture a vibrant community around the game, ultimately leading to a higher NPS.

To further strengthen the feedback loop, incorporating gamification strategies can spark ongoing player participation in the feedback process. Rewarding players with in-game currency, exclusive items, or experience points for sharing their thoughts not only spurs motivation but also cultivates a sense of ownership and connection to the game. By actively engaging players in the game's evolution, product managers can foster a devoted community that feels personally invested in the journey.

Lastly, leveraging influencer partnerships can significantly amplify the effectiveness of the feedback loop.

Influencers can champion the importance of player feedback and inspire their followers to join in surveys or discussions. By collaborating with influencers who are in line with the target audience, product managers can broaden their reach and capture a wider array of feedback. These influencers provide unique insights into player experiences, helping product managers refine their strategies. This holistic approach to establishing a feedback loop not only elevates player engagement but also drives higher NPS, paving the way for long-lasting success in the dynamic gaming industry.

Staying Ahead of Industry Trends

Staying on top of trends is not just important; it's essential for product managers in the video game sector who aspire to elevate their Net Promoter Score (NPS). By grasping the dynamic landscape of player preferences and technological innovations, product managers can adapt their strategies with agility and foresight. This proactive mindset not only retains loyal players but also attracts new enthusiasts, fueling growth and engagement. By continuously monitoring trends, managers unlock emerging opportunities and counter potential threats, ensuring they maintain a competitive edge in a fast-paced industry.

One of the most inspiring trends influencing player engagement is the growing demand for personalized experiences. Today's players yearn for games that speak to their unique preferences, making player feedback a cornerstone for product managers. Through systematic collection and insightful analysis of this feedback, managers can discover what players truly cherish. Infusing these insights into game design and updates sparks improvements in player satisfaction, driving a positive impact on NPS. Furthermore, harnessing advanced analytics tools empowers teams to predict future trends based on historical data, keeping them ahead of the curve.

In-game rewards and loyalty programs have emerged as powerful strategies for boosting player retention and satisfaction. As players seek acknowledgment for their dedication, thoughtfully designed loyalty programs cultivate a sense of belonging within the gaming community. Product managers should craft rewards that resonate deeply with their audience, such as exclusive content or in-game currency. By aligning these initiatives with player feedback, they can ensure relevance and desirability, encouraging players to dive deeper into the game and enhancing NPS.

Innovative gamification of feedback processes presents another exciting opportunity for product managers. By turning feedback mechanisms into engaging experiences, managers inspire players to share their thoughts enthusiastically. Integrating game-like features such as points, badges, or leaderboards transforms feedback collection into an enjoyable journey. This approach not only amplifies the volume of feedback received but also enriches the quality of insights gathered. As players invest in the feedback process, they view the brand as more attuned to their needs, further elevating NPS.

Lastly, influencer partnerships and marketing campaigns are vital for embracing industry trends with confidence. Collaborating with influencers who connect with the target audience enhances brand visibility and trust. Product managers should thoughtfully integrate these partnerships into their wider strategies aimed at enriching player engagement and satisfaction. By enlisting influencers to convey player feedback or highlight in-game rewards, companies create authentic connections with prospective players. This strategic alignment not only strengthens brand loyalty but can lead to remarkable improvements in NPS through heightened player advocacy and word-of-mouth marketing.

Let's embark on a journey to future-proof our NPS!

Future-proofing your Net Promoter Score (NPS) strategy is not just essential; it's an inspiring journey for product managers in the gaming industry striving to maintain a competitive edge. As the gaming landscape transforms, player expectations and engagement techniques evolve, too. An effective NPS strategy becomes a living entity, adaptable and forward-thinking, embracing current trends while anticipating the future of player behavior and preferences. This dynamic process requires a commitment to regular analysis of player feedback, keen awareness of market shifts, and the integration of innovative approaches that truly resonate with your target audience.

A cornerstone of this journey is leveraging player feedback analysis to shape your product roadmap. By establishing robust mechanisms for gathering and analyzing player insights, product managers can uncover patterns and emerging trends that directly influence user satisfaction. Creating dedicated channels for feedback—be it through surveys, forums, or in-game prompts—invites players to share their thoughts. Regularly reviewing this invaluable data sparks timely adjustments in gameplay features, ensuring the game remains not just relevant but truly enjoyable.

In-game rewards and loyalty programs are pivotal in elevating NPS. As players increasingly seek value beyond mere gameplay, incorporating meaningful rewards transforms their overall experience. Designing flexible loyalty programs that adapt to ever-changing player preferences and behaviors enriches their journey. By engaging players with personalized rewards tailored to their gaming habits, you cultivate satisfaction and foster a sense of community and belonging, significantly boosting their likelihood to recommend the game to others.

Embracing the gamification of feedback processes also opens a world of possibilities. By turning feedback collection into an engaging experience, you enhance player participation and ensure every voice is heard. Implementing gamified elements like challenges, leaderboards, or rewards for providing feedback invites players to join the conversation actively.

This not only enriches the quality and quantity of insights but also reinforces a positive bond between players and the game, contributing to an elevated NPS.

Finally, influencer partnerships and marketing campaigns can elevate your NPS strategy to new heights. Collaborating with influencers who truly resonate with your target audience amplifies your outreach and fosters new player engagement with your game. These influencers offer authentic feedback and insights that shape your development process while championing your brand. By weaving these partnerships into your NPS strategy, you cultivate a dynamic, responsive approach to player engagement, ensuring your game remains enticing in an ever-evolving market.